BEVERAGE TRUCKS
1910 THROUGH 1975
PHOTO ARCHIVE

BEVERAGE TRUCKS
1910 THROUGH 1975
PHOTO ARCHIVE

Donald F. Wood

Iconografix
Photo Archive Series

Iconografix
PO Box 609
Osceola, Wisconsin 54020 USA

Books in the Iconografix *Photo Archive Series* are offered at a discount when sold in quantity for promotional use. Businesses or organizations seeking details should write to the Marketing Department, Iconografix, at the above address.

Library of Congress Card Number 96-75229

ISBN 1-882256-60-3

97 98 99 00 01 02 03 5 4 3 2 1

Cover design by Lou Gordon, Osceola, Wisconsin

Printed in the United States of America

U.S. book trade distribution by Voyageur Press, Inc. (800) 888-9653

PREFACE

The histories of machines and mechanical gadgets are contained in the books, journals, correspondence, and personal papers stored in libraries and archives throughout the world. Written in tens of languages, covering thousands of subjects, the stories are recorded in millions of words.

Words are powerful. Yet, the impact of a single image, a photograph or an illustration, often relates more than dozens of pages of text. Fortunately, many of the libraries and archives that house the words also preserve the images.

In the *Photo Archive Series*, Iconografix reproduces photographs and illustrations selected from public and private collections. The images are chosen to tell a story—to capture the character of their subject. Reproduced as found, they are accompanied by the captions made available by the archive.

The *Iconografix Photo Archive Series* is dedicated to young and old alike, the enthusiast, the collector and anyone who, like us, is fascinated by "things" mechanical.

Dedicated to the memory of A.W. "Pop" Hays, founder of the Hays Antique Truck Museum, Woodland, California.

FOREWORD

Beverage bodies have long been a favorite of mine. They were the subject of some of my earliest truck articles, published over 20 years ago. The photographs of *Beverage Trucks 1910 through 1975 Photo Archive* are from many sources, and I thank them all.

Several persons support a fund at San Francisco State University that supports old truck research. We acknowledge some of the donors: Stuart B. Abraham, Edward C. Couderc of Sausalito Moving & Storage, Gilbert Hall, David Kiely, ROADSHOW, Gene Olson, Oshkosh Truck Foundation, Charlie Wacker, and Bill West.

Donald F. Wood
San Francisco State University
June 1996

An early 1930s International transporting Tip Top Whim.

INTRODUCTION

The term "beverage trucks" is fairly loose and can be applied to a truck carrying beverages of any type. An earlier term was "bottler's truck", which was more applicable at a time prior to the widespread use of aluminum cans. In this book, we shall look at trucks used to distribute beer, soft drinks, and bottled water.

Beverages are very heavy, mainly because of their high content of water. In the grocery business, during summer months, nearly half the weight of groceries handled is accounted for by beverages. Most bottling takes place in cities near to markets. Typically, bottlers employed driver/salesmen to make deliveries. Driver/salesmen had a regular route and would call on retail stores, leaving new stock and picking up empty bottles. (The driver/salesman's role in handling return bottles changed in the 1960s, as the use of no deposit-no return bottles and, later, recyclable containers increased.) He was responsible for the appearance of his product and would straighten and dust the display. He might make a small sales pitch to the retailer and would always try to get more shelf space or a display area at the end of an aisle. Large bottlers also had a separate sales force that would handle larger promotions. Their trucks would carry large display signs, which they would encourage a merchant to use.

Beverages were distributed in horse-drawn wagons, prior to the motor truck. However, because of their weight, the carriage of beverages was quickly transferred to motor trucks. Soft drink and beer bodies are nearly the same with one exception, beer bodies are generally enclosed. Enclosed bodies prevent thefts and protect beer from sunlight, especially damaging to unpasteurized beer. Some beer bodies also handle barrels and kegs. Barrels are heavy. A full barrel weighs 355 pounds. Insulated and refrigerated bodies were adapted to hauling beer, both to protect its unpasteurized state and to maintain a cool temperature for consumption.

The development of soft drink bodies has followed a steady progression, with trucks becoming larger and able to carry heavier loads. Early trucks were flatbeds. Later, shelves were added, each being high enough to hold case-lots of bottles. Often there was a slight inward tilt to the shelves that kept cases in place. Sometimes a two-wheel dolly would be kept on the roof. Cases of empties would also be placed on the roof until enough space became vacant on the shelves. The limits to height were those of the driver/salesman's reach. Initially, all of the load was higher than the frame. Eventually partial shelves were added at a lower level, one either side of the rear wheels.

During the 1930s, there was a considerable interest in streamlining beverage trucks. The art was carried to its extreme in Canada, where brewers used streamlined trucks as a form of advertising. Following World War II, however, designs were not as fancy. Trucks of greater and greater capacity were built and bottlers relied more on mechanical equipment for loading and unloading. The bays of trucks became much larger, to permit loading of palletized beverages by forklift or pallet jack. Today, large quantities of beverages move by semi-trailers. More deliveries are being made to the warehouses and distribution centers of large chain stores, which redistribute the beverages to their affiliates via their own trucks that also carry other merchandise.

Beverage bodies have traditionally not come with the truck. The bottler would buy a truck chassis and purchase a beverage body from a body builder. Sometimes the body would be shipped to the truck dealer, who would install it, or the chassis would be delivered to the body builder or his dealer for installation. The bodies were painted to match the truck's chassis and cab and would follow the fleet painting instructions of the bottler or brewer. Bottlers and brewers also supplied decals with their product names and logos. Many early beverage bodies also carried an advertising letter board at the top of the load, parallel to the truck.

Beverage trucks continue in widespread use today, although many are tractor and semi-trailer combinations. For better or worse, long gone are the days when smaller trucks and the driver/salesman made case-lot deliveries to Mom and Pop corner groceries.

Cases of Coca-Cola were loaded flat on the bed of this Rapid, with the row in the center being one case higher. The last rows were at an angle, supported by the flare boards.

A circa-1911 White, ready for a parade, carries barrels of Circle Brand Ginger Ale. A Dr. Pepper sign is also displayed. Circle Brands of Waco, Texas was first to bottle Dr. Pepper in about 1886.

12

A 1911 White carrying empty cases of Erin Brew.

An unknown make of truck, circa 1912, used by The Coca-Cola Company to carry signs and other promotional materials.

A fancy 1913 White used to distribute Pabst Beer in Cleveland, Ohio. Truck has pneumatic tires in front; solid tires in rear. Note artwork on rear panel.

An electric truck, circa 1915, used by Anheuser-Busch.

16

A 1915 White used in Galveston, Texas. The body looks as though it could be dumped, but this does not seem to be the appropriate time to find out. Load is tied down with ropes.

A Ford Model T, circa 1915. In rear is an enclosed cargo box.

The Franklin Brewery, Flushing Avenue, Brooklyn, New York, used this 1916 White.

A 1917 Hewitt owned by the Lion Brewery, New York City.

A 1919 Pierce-Arrow carrying Duquesne Beer, distributed by the Independent Brewing Co., Pittsburgh, Pennsylvania.

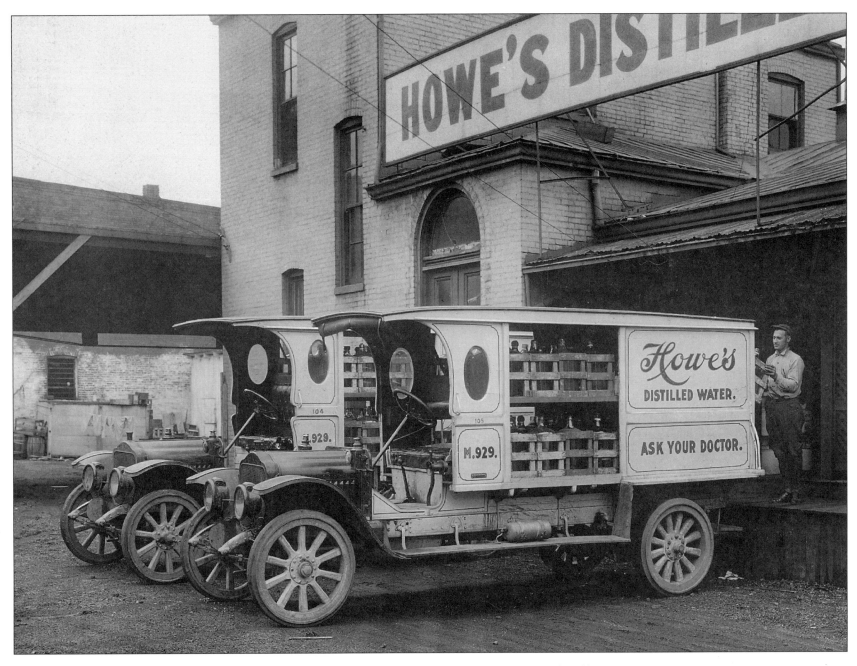

A pair of 1919 White trucks carrying bottled Howe's Distilled Water, Nashville, Tennessee.

Hendrickson trucks were made in Chicago, Illinois. This one, from about 1920, distributed Manhattan Ginger Ale.

A 1920 Corbitt, built in Henderson, North Carolina, with a Pepsi-Cola body.

A circa-1920 GMC, used in the Los Angeles area, with a load of spring water. A number of fruit flavors are painted along the floor of bed.

A 1921 REO.

No. 120—Bottlers' Delivery Wagon

A bottler would buy a truck chassis, which would be delivered to a truck body builder. The body builder would attach the body to the truck, paint it and deliver it to the bottler. Here, from a body builder's catalogue, we see (in dark shading) the cab and body designed to fit a Ford TT chassis.

Moreland trucks were built in Southern California. This one, from the early 1920s, carries Sierra Club Ginger Ale.

The Fort Smith, Arkansas Coca-Cola distributor has his fleet ready to participate in a parade in the early 1920s. Note striped pattern on hoods. Trucks carry flags, and at far right is a team of horses, hitched to a wagon. The blankets on the horses promotes Coca-Cola.

An early-1920s GMC with an enclosed load. Note snap-on device protecting driver from having to sit in an open cab.

A White tank truck, circa 1920, used for dispensing Coca-Cola by the glass. The drink is advertised as "Ice Cold" so there must be a device to keep the load chilled, probably separate compartments for ice.

An early-1920s Mack, with a C-cab, used by Coca-Cola in New Orleans, Louisiana.

An early-1920s Sterling.

The Dr. Pepper distributor in Dallas used this 1920s International. Cases are loaded in a level position.

A mid-1920s International used to distribute Dr. Pepper in Dallas, Texas. Note cases are tilted inward.

Both Coca-Cola trucks look new and have 1924 license plates. At right is a White with a conventional open beverage body. The small truck on the left is a REO and has "sales and advertising" painted on it. The sales manager would use it and call on merchants, encouraging them to devote additional space to product displays.

A mid-1920's Mack pulling a full trailer. Large cut-outs of Coke bottles are placed in each of the stake holes alongside the load. Trailer appears to have pneumatic tires, the truck does not.

The truck is probably a mid-1920s Nelson LeMoon and it's used to carry bulk Prima Beer to a bottling plant. Groen Manufacturing Co., Chicago built the tank.

A 1925 White with a roof, used to carry Moxie.

A 1928 White Deluxe long wheelbase panel.

A Ford AA carrying Alhambra drinking water.

A late-1920s White with a completely enclosed body with large side doors. Sign boards are on each side of roof and above cab. Note conveyor bringing cases from the bottling plant.

A 1929 White used in Baltimore, Maryland to distribute Suburban Club.

A 1930 White with semi-trailer plus a full trailer, used in Detroit, Michigan for hauling Vernon's Ginger Ale.

44

A small Coca-Cola bottling plant with its circa-1930 delivery fleet. From left to right: Chevrolet panel delivery, used by the sales manager; two Whites; a REO; two Fords.

A circa-1930 Chevrolet used in a parade by the Coca-Cola distributor in Wewoka, Oklahoma. Note model of an oil well sitting on top of the load.

A 1933 White with an enclosed body delivering Erin Brew to a restaurant in Cleveland, Ohio.

A 1932 White with a semi-trailer. Curvature in front allowed trailer to clear cab on turns, although it cut into space for placing cases. Note that the Coca-Cola is stored five cases high.

1933 Indiana stake truck used to distribute Stegmaier Gold Medal Beer in Wilkes Barre, Pennsylvania.

Unrolling a barrel of beer from an early-1930s International.

Unloading barrels of Dawes Beer from a 1933 White flatbed, Montreal, Quebec.

A mid-1930s International, used in Astoria, Oregon for distributing Acme Non-fattening Beer.

A driver in front of his load of Dr. Pepper. Truck is a 1934-35 Chevrolet.

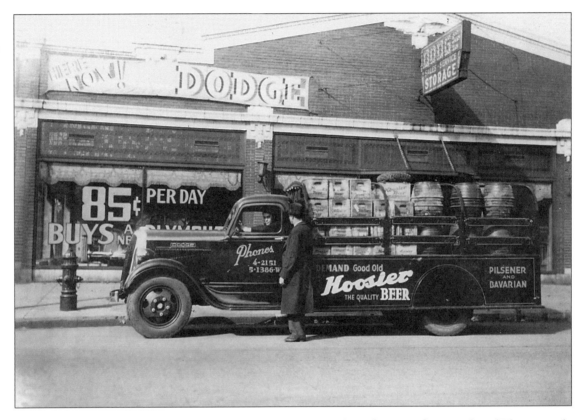

A 1935 Dodge carrying Hoosier Beer, parked in front of a Dodge/Plymouth dealer, whose window sign indicated that one can buy a new Plymouth at a cost of 85 cents a day.

A mid-1930s Mack with a stake body built for the Griesedieck Stag Beer Co., Belleview, Illinois.

A Kranz body on a 1936 Mack Junior chassis.

A 1935 Indiana used to carry Carlings Ale and Beer.

A fleet of six 1936 Dodges carrying Schepp's Blu-Bonet Lager. The brewery also has its "foam" number painted on the trucks.

A 1936 Studebaker with a streamlined stake body used by the Coca-Cola Bottling Co., Alliance, Ohio.

In the late 1930s, one way that Canadian brewers promoted their products was through the use of distinctively streamlined trucks. Count Alexis de Sacknoffsky designed this body for a 1936 White chassis.

A 1937 White carrying a Sacknoffsky-designed body.

Rear of a Trailmobile trailer used by the Burkhardt Brewing Co., Akron, Ohio.

American Body and Equipment Co., Dallas, Texas, built the body on this 1938 Chevrolet.

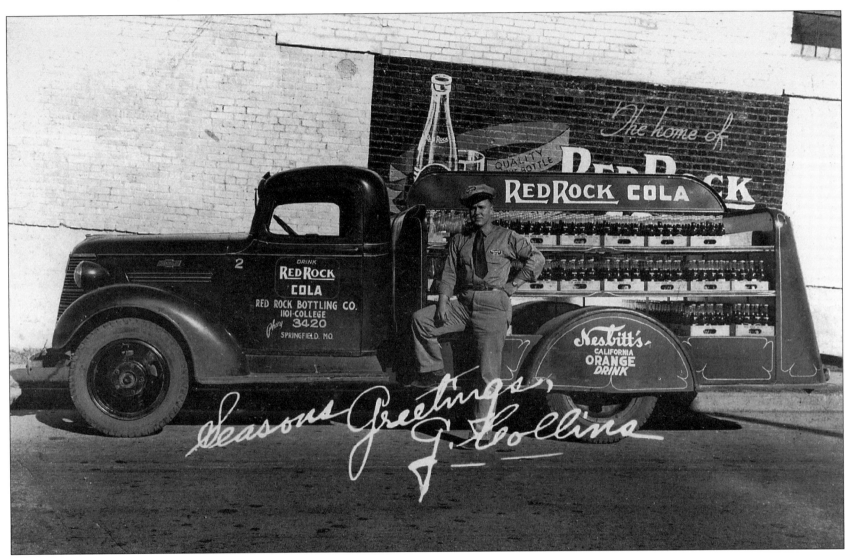

The distributor of Red Rock beverages, Springfield, Missouri, used this as a holiday greeting card. The truck is a 1938 Chevrolet.

A 1938 White stand-up van used in El Paso, Texas. It may have been used by a salesperson, and carried either promotional materials or a cooler.

This 1938 Dodge COE carried both soft drinks and beer. Note that part of the body was enclosed, which was used for beer, and part was open, used for the soft drinks. Empty wooden cases are carried on top. Brands of beer carried include Pioneer, Old Milwaukee, Acme, and Hop Gold.

Rheingold Beer barrels in a late-1930s Mack.

The body on this late-1930s White has enclosed compartments at the bottom, probably for beer.

The White Horse chassis was intended for step vans. This one was used for a small, enclosed Coca-Cola body.

A 1940 Ford with a Pepsi body.

A 1940 Chevrolet carrying a load of Dr. Pepper. Hackney Bros. Body Co., Wilson, North Carolina, built the body.

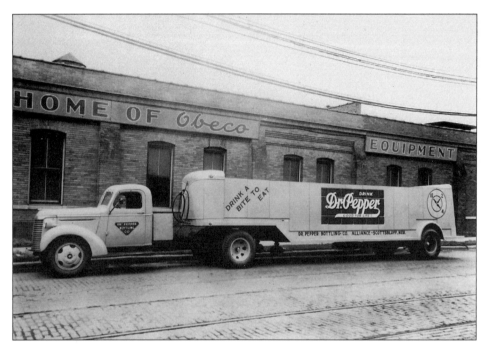

A 1940 Chevrolet tractor and semi-trailer used to distribute
Dr. Pepper in the vicinity of Scotts Bluff, Nebraska.

A custom body on a circa-1940 Dodge chassis, used to carry Miller Beer.

A Heiser beverage body on an early-1940s Dodge used to carry Par-T-Pak beverages.

A 1941 Ford was customized by having auto headlight rims turned 90 degrees. Grille is from a COE and the body was built by Kranz.

A 1941 GMC with bottled water.

A 1940s Autocar with a trailer designed to pneumatically transfer and carry grain for the brewer of Altes Lager Beer.

A mid-1940s Dodge delivering bottled water to an I. Magnin store in southern California.

Red Rock Cola carried in a 1940s Dodge. The beverage body was built by Schnabel of Pittsburgh.

A 1940s International with an enclosed stake body used to distribute Falstaff Beer in St. Charles, Missouri.

There's no doubt what this circa-1948 Chevrolet COE is carrying.

A 1948 Dodge tractor with a semi-trailer carrying Hartz Beer in the Pacific Northwest.

A 1948 GMC flatbed used for carrying bottled water in the Los Angeles area.

Note how high the single side panel lifts. Truck is a late-1940s Ford.

A 1948 Ford carrying Grapette.

A circa-1949 White used to distribute Old Export Beer in Cumberland, Maryland.

A late-1940s Chevrolet used in San Antonio, Texas. Note floor is designed so that cases tip slightly inward.

A late-1940s GMC truck and trailer carrying bottled water.

A body for carrying Canada Dry beverages has been completed and is ready for placement on a truck chassis. Note toeholds, rear step in front of lights, and diamond-tread metal, all of which are for use when reaching top deck. Driver/salesman often kept a two-wheel dolly on top deck. The picture is from the late 1940s.

Note roof over the open side. Truck is a late-1940s International.

Meister Brau carried inside a conventional body on a late-1940s REO chassis.

A customized GMC, circa-1950, used to carry bottled water. Note turn indicator arrow behind cab.

Side view of an enclosed beverage body on a circa-1950 Chevrolet COE. Triangular compartment in the rear is for carrying small fold-out displays to be given to retailers.

A circa-1950 White COE used by Coca-Cola in Atlanta. Note that it carries six levels of cases.

A circa-1950 Studebaker with a stand-up body used by 7UP.

A 1950 Chevrolet sedan delivery used by sales staff of Sicks' Select Beer, sold in the Pacific Northwest.

A circa-1950 GMC with a Heiser body, used in Everett, Washington to carry Squirt.

Side drawing of a beverage body designed to hold cases, circa 1950.
The body was designed by the Kolstad Co., Minneapolis, Minnesota.

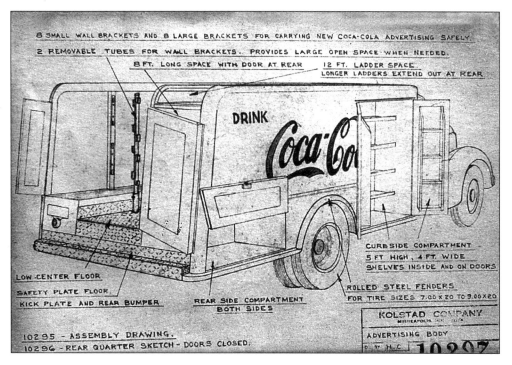

8 SMALL WALL BRACKETS AND 8 LARGE BRACKETS FOR CARRYING NEW COCA-COLA ADVERTISING SAFELY.

2 REMOVABLE TUBES FOR WALL BRACKETS. PROVIDES LARGE OPEN SPACE WHEN NEEDED.

8 FT. LONG SPACE WITH DOOR AT REAR   12 FT. LADDER SPACE
LONGER LADDERS EXTEND OUT AT REAR

DRINK

Coca-Col

CURB SIDE COMPARTMENT
5 FT HIGH, 4 FT. WIDE
SHELVES INSIDE AND ON DOORS

LOW CENTER FLOOR

SAFETY PLATE FLOOR

KICK PLATE AND REAR BUMPER

REAR SIDE COMPARTMENT
BOTH SIDES

ROLLED STEEL FENDERS
FOR TIRE SIZES 7.00 X 20 TO 9.00 X 20

KOLSTAD COMPANY
MINNEAPOLIS

ADVERTISING BODY

10297

10295 - ASSEMBLY DRAWING.
10296 - REAR QUARTER SKETCH - DOORS CLOSED.

A circa-1950 Kolstad advertising body used to carry in-store displays for Coca-Cola.

A Schnabel flatbed body on a 1952 Diamond T chassis that carried beer for the Pittsburgh Brewing Co.

Welding a Hesse beverage body, circa 1954.

A 1954 Ford, with a Mickey body, used to distribute Budweiser Beer in Winston-Salem, North Carolina.

Not exactly a beverage truck, but related. The tank truck on the street is pumping anti-freeze into the bubbling solution used in a giant Pepsi-Cola bottle display on top of a building in Times Square, New York, 1956.

Open bays in a Hesse body carried on a circa-1960 Chevrolet COE chassis.

A 1960 C.O.E. delivering Coca-Cola to a Delta Airlines jet, Miami International Airport.

Loading bottled water. Note that empty bottles are loaded on to
the truck and then filled.

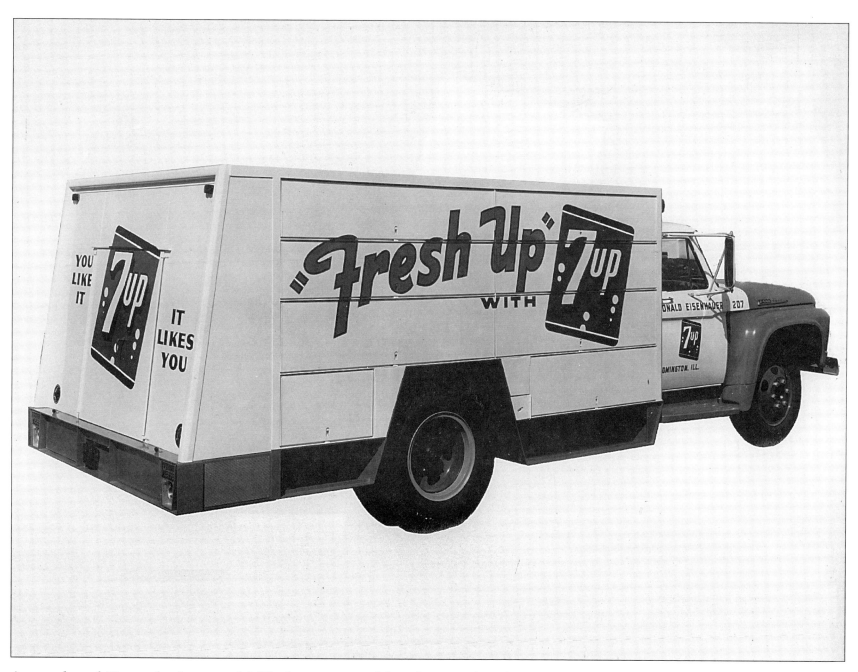

An enclosed Hesse body on a 1962 chassis, used by the 7UP bottler in Bloomington, Illinois.

A 1962 GMC with a Hesse open-bay body. Pallet-loads of soft drinks would be loaded an unloaded by forklift trucks.

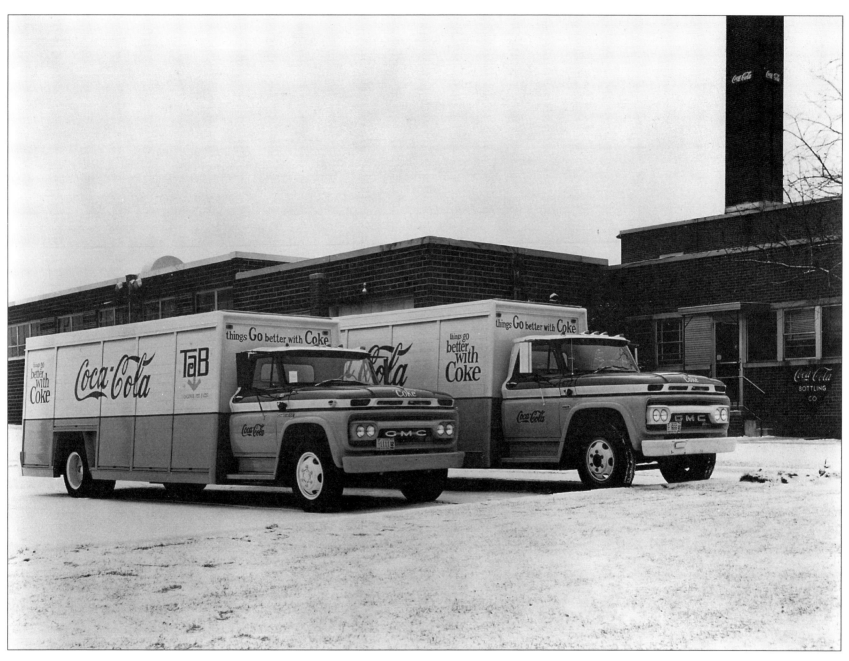

Two enclosed bodies on 1962-63 GMC chassis. Trucks have Iowa license plates.

This is a Hesse body on an early-1960s International. The front compartment could hold pallets or barrels. Compartment above rear wheels would hold cases.

This 1963 Ford, used to distribute Pepsi-cola in the vicinity of Springfield, Missouri, came in second.

A 1963-64 International with a refrigerated body for carrying draft beer in Kansas City, Missouri.

A mid-1960s Chevrolet chassis with Heiser body, carrying Ranier Beer for a distributor in Bremerton, Washington.

Circa-1964 Diamond T COE pulls a refrigerated tank trailer full of beer. The 5000-gallon body was built by Penske Tank Co.

Busch Bavarian Beer carried in a mid-1960s GMC, with a Hesse Body. The side panels lifted.

A mid-1960s GMC with a Heiser body, carrying Shasta soft drinks.

An enclosed Hesse body used to carry Hamm's Beer. Truck is a late 1960s Chevrolet.

Two views of a Hesse body on a circa-1970 GMC chassis.

A Ford C with a short-wheelbase trailer carrying Schlitz Beer.

An early-1970s International carrying Diet Rite Cola in a Hesse body.

A load of beverages is heavy. When an attempt was made to load this early-1970s beverage truck, its frame bent.

A Hesse body outfitted to carry Michelob Beer in barrels. Doors are insulated and truck body has a refrigeration device to keep the draft beer cooled.

A mid-1970s International COE with a Hesse body designed to carry 7UP.

A Hesse body on a mid-1970s GMC. It carries cases of 7UP. There are nine doors on this side.

A mid-1970s GMC with Kinnaird body carrying Royal Crown Cola. In front of driver's knee, a pallet is barely visible. A forklift truck loaded the bay with a pallet load five or six cases high. The driver is unloading case by case.

Photo Credits

COVER: GMC **PAGE 8**: Navistar Archives **PAGE 11**: THE COCA-COLA COMPANY **PAGE 12**: Dr. Pepper Co. **PAGE 13**: Volvo/White **PAGE 14**: THE COCA-COLA COMPANY **PAGE 15**: Volvo/White **PAGE 16**: Anheuser-Busch Archives **PAGE 17**: Volvo/White **PAGE 18**: THE COCA-COLA COMPANY **PAGE 19**: Volvo/White **PAGE 20**: Smithsonian Institution **PAGE 21**: University of Michigan **PAGE 22**: Volvo/White **PAGE 23**: Hendrickson Mfg. Co. **PAGE 24**: Free Library of Philadelphia, Pennsylvania **PAGE 25**: Arrowhead and Puritas Waters Inc. **PAGE 26**: The William F. Harrah Automobile Foundation **PAGE 28**: Gary Gollott **PAGE 29**: National Park Service, Fort Smith National Historic Site **PAGE 30**: The Coca-Cola Bottling Company of New York, Inc. **PAGE 31**: THE COCA-COLA COMPANY **PAGE 32**: THE COCA-COLA COMPANY **PAGE 33**: Western Reserve Library **PAGE 34**: Dr. Pepper Co. **PAGE 35**: Dr. Pepper Co., Dallas **PAGE 36**: The Coca-Cola Bottling Company of New York, Inc. **PAGE 37**: THE COCA-COLA COMPANY **PAGE 38**: American Automobile Manufacturers Association **PAGE 39**: Volvo/White **PAGE 40**: Volvo/White **PAGE 41**: FABCO **PAGE 42**: The Coca-Cola Bottling Company of New York, Inc. **PAGE 43**: Volvo/White **PAGE 44**: Volvo/White **PAGE 45**: Museum of the Albermarle **PAGE 46**: THE COCA-COLA COMPANY **PAGE 47**: Volvo/White **PAGE 48**: Volvo/White **PAGE 49**: Volvo/White **PAGE 50**: Navistar Archives **PAGE 51**: Volvo/White **PAGE 52**: New Haven Carriage & Auto Works, Portland, Oregon **PAGE 53**: Fort Bend County Museum, Texas **PAGE 54**: National Automotive History Collection, Detroit Public Library **PAGE 55**: McCabe-Powers Body Co. **PAGE 56**: Kranz Automotive Body Co. **PAGE 57**: Volvo/White **PAGE 58**: Chrysler Historical Collection **PAGE 59**: The Coca-Cola Bottling Company of New York, Inc. **PAGE 60**: Volvo/White **PAGE 61**: Volvo/White **PAGE 62**: Columbia Body & Equipment Co. **PAGE 63**: American Body & Equipment Co. **PAGE 64**: State Historical Society of Missouri **PAGE 65**: Volvo/White **PAGE 66**: Chrysler Historical Collection **PAGE 67**: American Automobile Manufacturers Association **PAGE 68**: Volvo/White **PAGE 69**: Volvo/White **PAGE 70**: Kranz Automotive Body Co. **PAGE 71**: Hackney Bros. Body Co. **PAGE 72**: Omaha Body & Equipment Co. **PAGE 73**: A. L. Hansen Mfg. Co. **PAGE 74**: Geo. Heiser Body Co. **PAGE 75**: Kranz Automotive Body Co. **PAGE 76**: Arrowhead and Puritas Waters Inc. **PAGE 77**: American Automobile Manufacturers Association **PAGE 78**: Arrowhead and Puritas Waters Inc. **PAGE 79**: Historical Society of Western Pennsylvania **PAGE 80**: Kranz Automotive Body Co. **PAGE 82**: Geo. Heiser Body Co. **PAGE 83**: Arrowhead and Puritas Waters Inc. **PAGE 84**: American Truck Historical Society **PAGE 86**: Volvo/White **PAGE 87**: Western Reserve Library **PAGE 88**: Arrowhead and Puritas Waters Inc. **PAGE 89**: Kolstad Company **PAGE 90**: Dailey Body Co. **PAGE 91**: General Body Company, Chicago **PAGE 93**: Kolstad Company **PAGE 94**: Volvo/White **PAGE 95**: Geo. Heiser Body Co. **PAGE 96**: Geo. Heiser Body Co. **PAGE 97**: Geo. Heiser Body Co. **PAGE 98**: Kolstad Company **PAGE 99**: Kolstad Company **PAGE 100**: Historical Society of Western Pennsylvania **PAGE 101**: Hesse Corporation **PAGE 102**: W. F. Mickey Body Co. **PAGE 103**: American Truck Historical Society **PAGE 104**: Hesse Corporation **PAGE 105**: Hesse Corporation **PAGE 106**: Black Mountain **PAGE 107**: Hesse Corporation **PAGE 108**: Hesse Corporation **PAGE 109**: Hesse Corporation **PAGE 110**: Hesse Corporation **PAGE 111**: Hesse Corporation **PAGE 113**: Geo. Heiser Body Co. **PAGE 114**: Penske Tank Co. **PAGE 115**: Hesse Corporation **PAGE 116**: Geo. Heiser Body Co. **PAGE 117**: Hesse Corporation **PAGE 118**: Hesse Corporation **PAGE 119**: Hesse Corporation **PAGE 120**: Hesse Corporation **PAGE 121**: Beer Wholesaler **PAGE 122**: Hesse Corporation **PAGE 123**: Hesse Corporation **PAGE 124**: Hesse Corporation **PAGE 125**: GMC

The Iconografix Photo Archive Series includes:

The Iconografix Photo Archive Series is available from direct mail specialty book dealers and bookstores worldwide, or can be ordered from the publisher. For additional information or to add your name to our mailing list contact:

Iconografix
PO Box 609/BK
Osceola, Wisconsin 54020 USA

Telephone: (715) 294-2792
(800) 289-3504 (USA)
Fax: (715) 294-3414

Book trade distribution by Voyageur Press, Inc., PO Box 338, Stillwater, Minnesota 55082 USA (800) 888-9653
European distribution by Midland Publishing Limited, 24 The Hollow, Earl Shilton, Leicester LE9 7N1 England

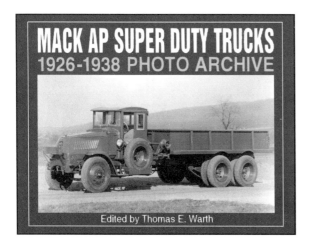

MACK AP SUPER DUTY TRUCKS
1926-1938 PHOTO ARCHIVE
Edited by Thomas E. Warth

MORE GREAT BOOKS FROM ICONOGRAFIX

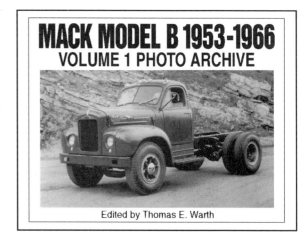

MACK MODEL B 1953-1966
VOLUME 1 PHOTO ARCHIVE
Edited by Thomas E. Warth

MACK AP SUPER DUTY TRUCKS 1926-1938 *Photo Archive* ISBN 1-882256-54-9

MACK MODEL B 1953-1966 VOLUME 1 *Photo Archive* ISBN 1-882256-19-0

LOGGING TRUCKS *1915-1970 Photo Archive* ISBN 1-882256-59-X

STUDEBAKER TRUCKS 1941-1964 *Photo Archive* ISBN 1-882256-41-7

GREAT NORTHERN RAILWAY 1945-1970 *Photo Archive* ISBN 1-882256-56-5

COCA-COLA: ITS VEHICLES IN PHOTO-GRAPHS 1930-1969 *Photo Archive* ISBN 1-882256-47-6

AMERICAN SERVICE STATIONS 1935-1943 *Photo Archive* ISBN 1-882256-27-1

LOGGING TRUCKS
1915-1970 PHOTO ARCHIVE
Donald F. Wood

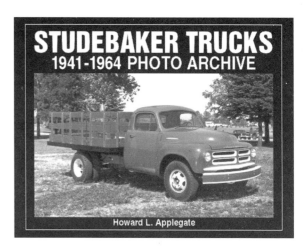

STUDEBAKER TRUCKS
1941-1964 PHOTO ARCHIVE
Howard L. Applegate

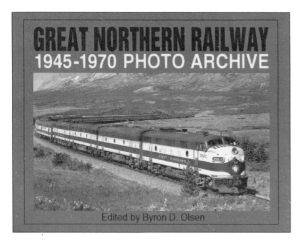

GREAT NORTHERN RAILWAY
1945-1970 PHOTO ARCHIVE
Edited by Byron D. Olsen

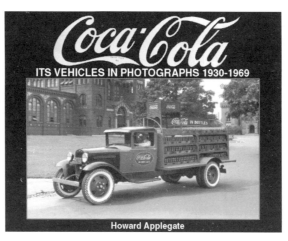

Coca-Cola
ITS VEHICLES IN PHOTOGRAPHS 1930-1969
Howard Applegate

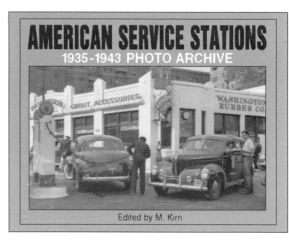

AMERICAN SERVICE STATIONS
1935-1943 PHOTO ARCHIVE
Edited by M. Kirn